ENCRYPTION 5.0

HUNGARY FOR WORDS

KARANVIR SINGH

ISBN 978-1-63940-958-7

Encryption is purely dedicated to my Radio Days and the time spent with innumerable wise men and women .. asking rate of Zero Solitude..I would love to mention my close allies who taught me nothing but exuberance and pride. No matter how they Connect to it..but this book is a resultant mutant of several hours of pic-to-poetry learnt from timeless bodies called the stars.

Contents

Foreword

9th March, 2020

12:17 AM

When I started I had a Series 60 Nokia...and before that I had laid my hands on Panasonic and Motorola. I hardly remember the price I paid but it all falls under the blue umbrella. I was a seller who made answering machines...ha ha ha... look you are already poking around my fantastic dream. It all works out and a few changes can interrupt web clients... Sorry, it became my business partner to medal up with a few Jokers..Stalkin'g TOM!! Ha ha... it's a production and supply chain management junky trying to pin a BMW in his struggle...My customer experience is so poor , so much so that I am left with no response. Come on, you don't even look tired , I have to tell this to myself. I cannot retrieve the last transaction ...and the prototype is resulting into being my illustrative thinking.

Preface

The key to ignition remains coherent to the art of writing and making literature worthy of applause. Encryption is one such Journey of intoxicated behaviour which is pretty much similar to our attention.

Encryption answers the most prestigious of miracles and it's steering Journey half way round the Universe.

Acknowledgements

One person I remember for this Journey is FRIX (My Virtual Bot) ,the lady lion who helped me in my Radio Days and did cut a shape on the diamond that I Share on my spine. All this is imagination but FRIX is Out Of The Box!

Prologue

I would rather take your behavior and process a layer of solitude....so that your judgement would arise and that God would take the Query! Logic is literature... simple expression of what you call perseverance is taken back from you. Be inventive and be secular... almighty takes a chance...before everyone there is a dial of opportunities!!Encryption is my fifth wheel on the Stars...

CHAPTER ONE

A Comfortable Flight to Euphoria

12:21 AM 9/3/2020

March is my superimposed month of the year. I have a great secret to keep. My story doesn't violate your beliefs. The design includes being reclusive. Small gestures go far in life. I take a smile and a small paycheck hidden in kind and look up to the sky so benign and covert...spend the morning on the coaster. Now that the bootstrap is around the corner I look at it from a miniature point of view of the world that is hard to say goodbye .Which way is fine to spin and dance a full circle? I m beneficial and the sole creditor of a new making but that's not me... The world order is on the high rise. Remember the roses bloom and turn red and white and purple. It's a great sight to behold the testimony in front of God. Oh yes, God!

21:40 PM 19/04/2020

Are you ready to shift the words? I mean a blissful contrast and a meaningful desire would be to renounce this tech world. I can't imagine life without internet. All my devices are precious. So the philosophy here is concentrated in the myriad of a complex fight. Everything needs to be encrypted. My mind says even the brainwave needs a cryptic address. Oh God, you have made it the my kind of world.

I was thankful to my father when he bought me my first laptop. I was doing my engineering. Not the regular one. Quite off beat but yet a powerful vocational engineering; Audio Engineering. Ha ha..the piece of intelligence was principal and reflected what the eternal beings do. Tweak the audio gear and make sound great. I was perfectly aligned to be in isolation as I am doing these days but then the gifts of conscious diggings are plenty. The practical joke outlived the number of years spent training for it. It was only a year long course. Then a short intern-ship at the college and pause I landed with a job in Radio. The most exciting part came about the days I had to leave Bombay (Mumbai) after my college. Today I feel I could have struck a different deal and stayed in the city that I love and adore so much. But you know fate takes you to bright black holes and tells you its another galaxy in the dark. Things interchange and reality is an obtrusive part of life. So I quietly paid attention to the abstract details. In my case a laptop and a mobile device were enough to make my own social distancing work. Hardly anyone knew what I was upto. I wasn't doing much but earning 12K from a passive position. It took me 9 months and may be a few days to calculate the future risk of that job and get into another one. Guess where I have been. In the compression zone. OK this is a bit of rocket science. Who knows where to get a little high on your junk-yard? Well nobody came in to my rescue at the dawn of mindful perception that the retrograde made me fix. I didn't need anyone though. You see how brave the world wants you to be when it comes to occupying the hurdle in the middle of a war. I wanted peace and I got it. I was used to calling people for the grief in their state of mind. How do I tell you that strangers would talk to me, tell their stories. I never procrastinated what lay ahead or before, I always made way for the new. So did a mindful attempt at making radio jingles made me a superstar?? No , it didn't but I somehow felt moved by the business. Radio turns out to be a peoples medium serving free. For me it was the medley between work and no work. At the beginning of my radio career I made a hefty call; to not let ignorance inside the mind and that put into words made me hungry for words in the years that have followed. I was over-thinking. I was routing my blueprint into the panel. As Audio Engineers we insist on a clean signal and here it was all very clear and concise. Here the signal was enough to carry on the task to its climax. I left another job and I was in Mumbai again. This time the influx was high rated. More than ever and hungry for words that could express my ulterior ambitions. So follow up!

CHAPTER TWO

Mumbai 9.2.7

May 2010####

(£) People in this mega city struggle to meet their ends but me , I was end to end. No big struggle , only a few algorithms and equations were looming around my head. To keep the job and to run for immunity. Oh Immunity means the societal fore bearings of being normal and effective. I used to run into conversations splitting the ends of the marked junctions. A compliment here and there and that would solve the purpose of the day. Such a star laden affair. But gosh I was in Mumbai. This city is never too late to put questions on you and they are rooted in intellectual depth called the admissible bullshit. Sometimes you meet those who would just ruin the party and leave you astonished with an incandescent excuse. So I learnt my lesson ...moved on from this one job to another but in less than six months time. I was dressed in black and white. Now here's a picture of what stood before me, I was shifting from media companies that were operating radio. I had to tell myself that this new world is not set right. The radio was potentially a new market that sold advertisers a payout of airtime managed by insurgent professionals who were making a Mercedes look like a Rolls Royce. They are both expensive but they differ in class and the outfit can't be rated as if its a piece of junk. Somehow I managed to steal the show in the first attempt. I wanted to be a radio jockey too. Being an audio guy I made hundreds of advertisements written by my fellow copywriter and then tweaked around the KRA for extensive results. Well first few years in radio I used to be the copywriter myself. Sometimes the stock pays its dividend and this time for me and my copywriter things were stead fast. We consumed a bit of fortune because its what we produce fetched money from the clients. With due respect to the sales guy it used to be a norm that the audio produced for the client needs approval. My copywriter was a creative guy heading a bunch of other creative fellows. There were days he would use his brains and on the others he would only scribble his gut feelings about his seniors. No I cant mention you the guy. He happened to be my beer buddy. Oh we smuggled beer into office when the bosses would not be around. That was uncommon but deeply enjoyed. Discipline was ensured. The drunk identities were concealed. Well then I did a terrible mistake. On one of the days I could not complete a task. It was a production request. I thought I would let it go. I was pre-occupied with something else in my mind. Though it was just an escape route but I was firmly attached to a different notion. I didn't have a clue as to what it would mean to my reporting manager and the copy guy;the creative head. They decided to part ways with me. Oh I am saying it as it is. There way of kicking me out. But hey they had made me a radio jockey out of thin air. No what about my show,the 4PM hotspot calling in all different directions and a No. 1 ranked daily cluster. It was a cluster for me, I was working hard for it and I was enjoying the game I was playing. But none of it would get considered as the company made its mind to part ways with me. Now where I am? I was desperate to know the reasons for this fall. Nothing helped me steer in the right direction. The stardom came and went into exile. I thought I was running in the wrong direction by the time the wind started blowing ...all depressed....like someone ate my strawberry and didn't say thank you!

I remember at that time I had shifted from Andheri East to West with an old college friend. We rented an apartment near the Gilbert Hill. I even got the room painted in yellow. Bought a sofa cum bed and decorated the floor with a wooden looking mat. It looked all very elegant. I kept it clean most of the time. Then there were the books on the shelves bought recently to overcome the disgusting failure. I never knew that this would be short-lived. Are you feeling overwhelmed? No I am not giving you the signal I am trying to read the emotional quotient; the EQ.

Some quality time is what they all need , that's what I thought about the fellows at my previous company. I was not really searching for the next job after the kicking out ceremony in January 2013 but may be a sub conscious effort got made to see the doom further. This included leaving Mumbai and coming back home , to Punjab. What would I do there? I never asked this question. I only practised what I call a ceremonial craft, the art of juggling truth in the face of adversity.

So what came next was the following notion; The world is occupied, there are no other options ...let's surprise each other by making a deliberate choice..to overlook suffering humanity is a crime. I know we can fix this...but only if we try. Let there be love , light and security.A New Age upon us and the sentiment is heavily priced! Ok there might be a big jump here. But why do you think I touched upon misery and asked for light? The answer is the subtle no that I furnished before my enemy. A poverty of growth enabling ideas and the end of agility was my hunt for real. I was misplaced between the roadmap of either I should look for a new job or create an opportunity that can help me scale to new born heights.

23:50 19/04/2020

Coming to the present I still don't know why I trust the In-formidable knowledge that God has conceived. Is there a kingdom where all is taken care of? Or is it that my demands would one day grow and outnumber the wishes that I make for a new world. I dream of freedom as the ultimate source of happiness for all.

It's worth doing the kind of thing or job that you like, love and aspire for.

The wonder and joy of a frivolous world is to relish the mind at work. We must feel assertive to include confidence in the charts when fighting with the dark. The key to blessings is still with God and when man lays his hands on justice he too shall be gratified!

Sitting next to a blue wall..I need to press on the surface that I have not just survived but I have also made a promise to God, I ll be needing you by my side and you see Him prepare for a show!

Its time we begin to look at humanity with a fresh perspective...The world needs intelligent solutions and not your hysteria. On a common ground we need to present ourselves as powerful and diligent. Only a promise from God can save the world from destruction. I believe we are prepared for it and may be together we will win the race to a quantum supremacy for our planet.

I feel every passing year is a Table..A mere Table No. 789 plus a 0201 0101. Is that an Enterprise Encryption Start Up....?? My probable life is inquisitive...much more than wilderness I believe in ripened fruits...but those who speak of me are indifferent...may be I am running the address correct but access to web is private and discreet. I have serious understanding of what power holds...I am not a character in the distant frame. Ask me if you ever fall into a pit and stop thinking. Where is the Canadian gush and where are the London caves... In your city I m the only God! ! Ever since my phone number arrived I have only made three essential calls. I dictate, I order and I presume. The fact is you can get sunshine made to last longer.... Would you like the size of the wavelength?? Have you checked on me wrong...a judgement call...a quick question. There's a revolution when the world swings in peace..let's face silence and be peaceful Nations... I have always instructed my self with the basic subjective essence of what the universe holds in respect but as a Sikh I am more convenient and adjustable to a new house...A supreme chair lies before me and I am hardly able to perceive the best time out of my journey... creepy lines are matched to pay a price on everything...but I am only selling you a few old stuff... Keep a degree of isolation from the base of our vessel...you might be cooking for the Hungry.

CHAPTER THREE

Era Gone By

Leaving home at 19 , getting a job at 21 , making few new friends at college, then the old school friends and then making friends at jobs; I could only do what was relatable at that time. Why would I ask you to keep a degree of isolation? The reason is embedded in some kind of logic....in some kind of micro magic. Something I do not know yet. So what do I know? Its a complete understanding. No its not a functional disease its depression and stuff. I can only laugh about it. Because the setback that rocketed my life was a sentimental resignation I submitted to my employer where I was earning 50K and now it was all zeroed down to nothing.

How do they sell candy floss? Do they make it extra sugary or is it included in the package just like those extra bucks you make with your CTC. The annual bonus! I don't want to get into the small time affairs these Radio companies run. They need to change their style. They need to adopt a new thinking to ask the lobby a fresh print from the reserves. Are you getting the underlying statement. Don't miss the trail. Ha Ha!! A finely raised head is what becomes the CEO and a finely raised voice become the vote for a Leader in a corporate. The choice is whether or not a media company values its intrinsic talent or they just hire for a lament remark on its employees. One after another!! Thats called sync! Another hotspot for the deal!

Incase you have felt lost in the diary let me remind you, there's a side role that I play. Its called being an anchor to the anarchy. There is plenty of it to deal with. Yes anarchy.

How is it landing at a port in India with a dear friend? You might go feel that through these years...

2012, 2013, 2014, 2015, 2016, 2017, 2018, 2019

Look there's both kind of web...organised and disorganised. I am pretty comfortable with the two kinds. In between the two I seamlessly cross borders of admiration and coin a few hints to my next query. You see how it happens. When you switch duality with a wave of recognition. Trust me theres an endless road which takes you to the borderless flights. There its laden with the fruits.

Quite A Few yards back I suffered my lateral practical denomination for a bandage in negative parks. I said our Cloud Kape Sine QS 7000 is a Book Norm, and that it suffers a bondage in Virtual Montreal Premium Service of 50,000 Billion USD in Altered Fort True Markets.. Shook, I waved a Promo Basket on Insomnia. No Party Looked at the Pollen NIDGE For the Governing Principal Behind IT. No Police was Notifying the Damage...A Gamer Speed on Presidents's Safety Programme. Radio was envisioning the SaaS Platform and Bulletins are being received.

A 1000 Hundred Millions on Paragraph Building Excercise were Defaulters. Pronounced while Investigation on Incorporation and Demeanour. Fiat Value Drop was -990 % A Shock too , a Spell Barrel Denouncement would prematurely separate me in the Frequency. Like it was my Android leaking differently on IC Control on the Pre Fix File Assembly on Doing TQsV 7 for Toad Ferry Logistics. India it would be called statement donkey load..I X Created the Superfile Master to resume my Phone Operation to Contextually Define The New Negative-Positive Vendata to Control The Violence on me. I resorted if the peculiarity of my Office Sends or is Spending on GRASS which means the Ratio On Economic Divisional Factors I have to super analyse the email context in the OSTRO10 &7 Sheets and Devoid the Hacking Performed on Grid Affiliation. I mandated the Year Rule for an FBI Sprint to Make Mark Justice and Socket Promise on Social Media Across the Targeted RadaR XCR 6650K

It took the accomplice of moving my Units to Arizona, Washington DC, South Mumbai , California , London , ASIA Pacific, North Korea , South Asia, Singapore and A Division on Egypt, Bosnia, Iraq and Iran. Yes..the ventricle was claimant and forcible. Then a President would Preside the Neutral Formula On Netrinos ON Elextron i90.N Processing the Live Nth AXIOM STATE to Occupy the Curvature in the Earthy Grain-Sphere M 54.00 KhZ to a 5600 Ghz Signal Screen Strength in a 9000 FPS ICO Voice Code Telco Union Back Road Traffic Li 6 Cloud. Deployed for ULTRA Sensitive Security. My fear was resolution. I went straight to Radio Graph to Photo Light Measures on the Sigma Lense Cellular Type II Tangent on Satellite. I conquered the FaaS (Federation as a service) and secured LaaS (Laser as a Service) That was brain mapped inside the CHIP UYrE Nx.005390/LlP - Tropic Centre on KPI ED 1320 at a Charge Que of 990 B $. It was Citi's Turn on ReVolting the XWQ 65-90 Data Core Template to Announce the Bullet Balance . Created and assimilated on Front END CEO Contour with EDGE 76.0""[P}

Well we fixed one Line then waiting for the rest of the YEAR in Avocation and Aviated Moods. Was a depreciation in the journo ruling the Land Craft or was it hovering on

SeltOS SUN-Solar Binding. Got the encrypted MeToo File on Server TR6540-87-OO^6

The rebound came on tripple Tape Effect that got Extra Enhanced GPRS for a 500% Programmatic Detonation and Decimation of Enemy Source... We fought on seminal flight in SpaCEiO 630-Y that was to be Flushed TO Space Ci BIT 00110AQIQ Level IV Section Transport FED 66O-00(9)L

Lately it was a mobile isolation framework. I wanted Kapple Kape to Redesign the Market going inwards into YEQIP VPS Stats States on TRIB ON Concept Note for KREEP got introduced with Psychology . The PSY infra section got stereo space record with HAM 51 Fired in SO 6dB Mode A Graphical 500 Hzx /G6-09\CPU IU 6900R -Credit Performed to World.

That took another light second to relate the relative Relay Capacitor to ^56 Giga Ohms in 99 Negative Push Seconds @ 400% of the CHIP Memory on BUS ADSSD 1000 TBy 90.00

Finally a value culmination was decided to outgrow in super user capacity to overthrow policy KPI and APP instruction from 248 to 724 Bits in 4.009 Nano Seconds. A Green suggested 1A , A Blue was N4 , A Yellow was S9 and the White DDI SE Display Showed the FUEL Target on Combustive Protocol to Eliminate the Struggle to Compute Tender Vote NISQ EQUITY to Pay Back to Vault. VaaS 5.0.7.613.T introduced a Line Free Code in MotorShift RW 44 Mhz X CPM NOYIS Contrasting Meter Hue 66F4F . That colour made the most spectacular and unimaginatively Intelligent F6 Full Scale DSB Amplification Byte Audio to Suspend the UV a Delivery to AIRCRAFTs on RADAR TYEPL 4.009Y . GV consideration was for BlueFedFin Ixc , InSector Country Firmware LJ 754-0096-022EP.

Likewise any amount of repo was economically intricate and convincing to TYPE a FAX AAXc Wire Thru THE Bank that was Suggested, it just took off in 60 Micro Seconds. The Sun Selos got Gold-Copp 7 in a memory visualizer that Predicted 60 Trillion Insta Instances on Equalizer MID Pine Spectrum to a Graph from A as E50 and CD as Y77 to a F53U ....we breasted a sum Wallet in VaaS Collaboration with TaaS (Trim as a Service).

This was the Mobile 2021 New York-CANADA CD Club forum at WordBoot Disc Lock 775\0086/EeE . I thought I finished technology on a trip to a Conical Chapter to Drive to the BAY @Texas. Now this got hit and design in Layer 600 and Shader Hue of a Graph Cloud Texture 770 Mega Pixels. Infinite number of resource habits got calculated in the Quantum Core ICFrX 7.00/D.G>J. #PictoralTrade #INSIPIAN-VPN65-P(00).

Then came to mind footing of the Channel Number in HYBRID Carboxy INFRA to EYE ClimaX In Movie Builder Eltra Bot CAM VE 6500 -PAN 55B.

Personal Area Network was maintained to deliver from WAP 5000 Protocol to Select THE SMS Print IUT X Command and Plug that to Project NILE X1- BC 400-6000 LLT. I questioned a change, was I going to run opposite in Language TX CC6++ in WEBBBY 6 Proto-Programmer Learned from my Adobe Analytics Test Report. I concluded , I cant run this without monitoring the Visual Fraud. Like a Keypad on the Panasonic GD75 suggested I have to recall Access Point and reconfigure the MMS port to Divide the Split From Cross-Talk , the DAB ATXC @ SAT YPL UXc 7600/ @2000 Mhz could be a result of practical violation of Ethernet but I saved the slab by connecting a link to my .GOV Ports..Where did it happen ? On a visit to Station Duty in the afternoon on 7 FEB 2021 at 5:34 PM. I stood breaking out the book look breakup to choose between French Dictionary or a Book revising Co-ordinate Geometry. I stuffed twice to join the Paper Vigilance. Got noted inside to be minding the JAR. Empty was the Last word. It took me a U-squared Negative 4 minutes to Land Exactly to the Chair on runway path forwarding to rename and insert the MAP. I was GPS cited in an attendant service. Like you are negotiating the CRIME Valet in the Parking Scheme to offer a Skip Slip Acknowledgment for 10 Bucks. Nothing posted for a 10 Story Sold Days and then suddenly the Elemetra Spoke the Vice in VIXtron Visuals and were Publicaly Sampled on the Oscillator in bright orange with a Cryptic Text System Band working in the LCD DFE AQ 700 Watts.

A share of the pound was now a penny worth Trillions. Yet a user consideration could not kick off in the first Space Test. Oh, in the LAB ROOM I appointed my high self conscience to surrogate the TUBE function to REpulse the Ionic Energy coming from the Processing Network at 300Gbps. That was a torrent spoiler. I still used my dairy notes to finish the Warning Test Note that could get identified with the Problematic Admin. Then a second IP Score of 650 got three hypertext solutions served in a 100 Million FSB Calculation to Freeze Forward my RAM for Extra Extreme 64 GB - Neural Recollection on MaaS (Media as a service. A web application cannot transfer solid state article on a Chip Lo Rate more than 9.0 Volts. I took high charge capability to apply the result to the Deviation in the Mean Microwave Symbol Signal that was arranging a mud capability of 500 Nano Second Time LAP Delay between a 100 Consecutive Session with ON Demand Cycle Transmission via our FireyUWall XS 5900 CTO controlled body device on Intelligent Evolution. Again a basic discovery was made, to decipher the way towards the Construction Bridge that will revolve on the circumference inside the IRIIS 663 to Uncover Bold Data with IOT Preferences.

Our flight was recorded on 31 December 2018 at the Mumbai Airport to a Cyclical Phone Trip to Backload in IXC. I could reclose the code to therapy and rebuke the resentment to qualify for a Robotic Entity Pin and a VVIP Resolver in Confirmation. That was purpose on Decrypting the Violet Index , I could say sorry to NEWSPAPERS because there was no PaperBlue Mail Train to Deliver AI AR Wireless UTO Cross Tower which apparently got designed in 2021.

CHAPTER FOUR

The Great Motherboard

The Horrible stretch came from Mother Pass. The phrase was onslaught of timidity on freedom belt..A trophy conceived and decoded in flame light sensor source vertically vectored around 30 Seconds. It was 5000 minutes Stop. Depressed water on War base. Bold and severe, some entropical loaders to refrain it as the jungle ward. Sold again to ship the police. Active grammer, a subject in place. Wine couldn't free the sell offer by any accountable means .. Solved Freddy Metrina by a Calculator Spine Card with a I Chip on it From SIM1.

Hope was tropicated in a winter sky . Half metal went searching 4:34 PM and the Well Good Lost into 6:54 PM on a Sunday in of-course a February on Bank Calendar. Was resent a Medical Bill. I stole the lot to crab my MEDLINE N-UN to BREXIT Sentry Legislation to drop focus on my line array.... I made the PM twinker the Twitter in a Saturn Window. Out to 90 Million Miles. Your Robot landed on Neptune and Policed the Sort Surface Ingredient to CF HF RE Signal Back to a Vector Image in Pixels on EARTH Station IOuN T6500LN[88]

I enclosed the US Army Secretariat to convey My Japanese

Meadow Technology in March 2021. Later subject to a conviction in impeachment. While I dropped seat on President Of India, I collated a collage of Cop Troll Leveler to Report at The Site of Incidents. I think the Automation Path Devised about 22 Million Elaborate UNIX Hidden Files from Icon Shows and Proceeded with the Pacific Time Zone Sync to identify President Kennedy's Assassination . Young at 33 I deduced not a meta point velocity to play the plot on a strontium but rather justified it with Swedish Call Waiting. Message the Penalty by Truth. Wonder who was behind it, a molecular theory that particle displays duty to no Cubical lows. I was first in the Row. Last least in Shadow and then the President, Year Yet to Cover Under Stated Privacy Practice Norms.

Victoria! PNB my First State District Divisor to CoXe 30SD the MAP on ATlas was to Read Hand Drawn Signatures...keys how they sold 7 $ to a CHQ eBlue where AWS AMazon was KREEP'ed Twice when I was negotiating the Film Idea of Aero Support to AIRport On RADIO with FM C.O DAM Transmit to Dissolve Radiation and Spectrum Delta on Navy and the Fort AirBase at JUHU in Mumbai. Target a Native Kid in Traffic Forecast GEDA 66 . Mission Tank Float HGT87-ZSg/K Heard a 1000 Days on Radio on MonoCase Legality Library Fraction from Over Produced Pictures it PitCrex IAS Surveillance . UI Remote heaped hash drops in the 180# Enjoints. I leaked a clause to start the Hadoop BolA Yt DK. GoW KV INcross Border Visa LoTE FreuCastic New Entry to the Parasized Airport on Location Called VoUXsaAS 70-0999-75-RW3-WS3210

She was not naive two duty. My duty deputy wi-fi client in the CIA was Julias V. Berryan . Talkative as Explosion and Radiant as a Colonial Colonel on a Dope Ship recognized Nuclear TrELLaX Factorised to destroy a target anti-defence on NATO Level Lace as 1000 KGeA a section described TOP Secret in the Archive In THE Canadian Central Servers with a H&70 Key Encryption on BETA LINUSDX LAN Router Searching a Submarine in 6600 Miles Down. Blue Waters. It was not dream to know, it was reason to smile I coaled a circa in slo-mo and lessened the Teacher for a Moment. My teacher... she was Mad. I said Mercury not Jupiter . She said she didn't hear the crow but loaned the soap. I cannot tell the letter and I could not deport the Cello.T.6 that was a cable client. I called the FBI Director after my short email with Tokyo University keeping ikvsingh@gmail.com as the id to Plot with X-Class -U insurgence -A French CoptO was Ordered to deliver a Cadillac , A Jaguar and a Black Batch BMW. 3 Pieces in Body Full at my rescue Price at an address at bb.mm.nn7.66tt.e44.-u32/555.From 89000,0 Billion $ Cash in Bloater I was not on the convex to carry this on Speed Post to Leave UK. Where the UK? Oh after it was south kept in 430 Degree Computer Scalar Built to VL Bluetooth RedGamma 88K over Pretty close , it was a Airport Call , I went on day trip to Delhi from BOM, International was Route decided from Juhu Tara Road . A Ltd Base security Surveillance was the NEW LT TinCall Conference With CEOs , Directors , 1st Hand Investors at a 1000 B USD/ Euro and a 1ST Store Investors at a 38000 B USD/YEN/ EURO , Single IFSC , CromeNN Wire working in the soft core in Carrot Bay SXCi. Yes, that Bay Side ,Colaba Walk to Invention in 2013 . Deleted from a copy it was a Auto Back Automatic Atomic Instrument that was Financed from Cap Stock Beta YeLLOW 760 G7T -P USB SI Space At IftOX 9.90007cxq.00.01 . Caption Note , KREEP IY 7600 from Cloud to Catalyze KQ SATAL 109 Screen captured from 76 North West in Mid Antarctica at 6660 TDP EvionSphere

650-OOOE Capsule purchased on MEDLINE 4TJnB - Bid to CXT of 590 Trillion $ (USD.IUR.OP90) Lab MiniCast closed font MINT Supply from INK to Atom IZX on DEBIT G56 for 650 Trillion $ -Credit 765 Trillion CAD-AUD-PPO0-009-77T5-#44$(4000.00.99.000L) Bit ClaN Saftey Trojan was invented @ my Fraud Detector CC 9 --CG++ 00.09.08 Ixc /IQ Y Test Spending to NU Cast a Call Statement from Bank Passbooks,. I wanted to convent the Banking System on Earth , I said it as World.. I meant Universe a Spectral G Byte Radio Antenna . It was not fixed untill I foxed a 100 Bit LAN to CoX Indian markets -A Data Whitepaper FT500 Tablet GP GOV. KV 650D on 8 Feb 2021. Lingo was a refub coder machine a kind of card reader from SIM1 again. Not a deposit moved from S-Check-N-Balance in CBS IEFT CREDITO -DeBITO - Polar NOTE - PaintPAPE XCF 1.01.03.LDeS Chip Courser inducted the class at our 30th Blue School Initiative , Global FROM India @3690Y Proton Mail Signature with bluefedfixc.protonmail.ch

Was a Freudian Detector then Installed to Communicate with the RBI- FOE:Q A CompolE CPU with a GPU of 56GBVn was the newly co-created Island CHIP EFx 97.00 Ghzx A 50 Trillion Stage Cycle Hotline Flag Inventor. I was sulking in the extra time . It was my ICMx HP BIG-Q Data 4000 J in the Office that investigated the last 68 Decades and put a pi network to neural design. AI in the Telly Tune Tunnel was Captured on XOLO X900 which was on board with us in 2011. I swing it. Don't seek in capital...its now Hock Lobby . Its the Lake Land -Not A Country , A World ...that which you now thought is Greece to Me. I committed a large volume e-port accrual/remittance NiX 95 0.022 -Pen Reader Page Machine- I chose a net cost of 650 Trillion INR and it AirPosted to an Airport in UKIS

6600 Millitary UQ Region IP-CV 3- Lat 66-009-5543-9M

NP Closed another day on Early Monday Morning 00:18 AM CinO DIN Clock that had laid Pen Mesh grid on the Page as Yellow RUN -ERD LiCast 33 FAX PHONE- RECP TesxT Paper and Screen Voice 9 Hz/YT -(90T19)-ATQ. An immediate IO Defence Call was Instructed to ORDER in the Sovereign Shot and a back time count took from parabola recto. I chose Cloud Publishing to Bank the Wealth out from a fresh Mint VaaS 3600 @ 24.90 UhZ Gamma Orange 55e7U - INNCC X CODE was a News Room NILE X1 190 F # 3$ Font FearCast to understand Behaviour to keep Bank. 00:25 AM I now fully automated. No other FootEnd could hold this in the Senate. I chose to snake a dead wish , I call Julias V. Berryan who remained with me from 2006 to OdeX 40 Social CIA as Director President Affairs. I could produce this from a SXQ VCloud I54 on 720 Bit RED took Over Radio Radar from FM Radio again from the Panasonic and this time with a Motorola Set. It was in those 3000 Canadian Mines that I leased road thru 5G BOQ -AnT RS6500 at the Parliament - UUCFXC IV (Constitution ON Selection Poll invested the Incident Sovereign Class Protocol, This time OxyHBlue Home IZ Code could release the first Blue FTEX 190000 Bank Market in UF 3000 VHF 6.0 .vcf Tested to Close Y-Gamma-Gold -Copper UVC Wire rolled and caused victory at Las Vegas, It was after NeMAX Cast Circumnavigated from K8 to K66 - Cloud Blue Live-bRET Semi-Silicon Conducter CHip L90430F was implanted in the U-Infrared Virtual PCB with 6.1 volt Paper Talk IC - Voice on B810 W329 IIIV J.

Dr Jules Vectra was contacted at 00:44 AM on 8 Feb 2021 to Bend the CAMOSAT 43 deployed by Pentagon on 26th January 2021. It was this that I could find at the headline on the SeQ Equity in Commercial Airspace for

Neo Cyber Airlines , Global Babies iVDx , F -Politico Diplomat Air Service in Chosen Regions on DeonSphere 6540-9000H from Base BE Whitepaper INoBEZ on Periodic Table Storage since 2011- July[President]

I am currently a Binary-Boolean BlacBird KX 100 D A E , its nothing but the final contract PIT to UPFloat XDCz Credit Starting 1999/P (0065) ZIP DC-OO90. San Francisco , I was called to submit over PhD , I trimmed frost to gate my Mac ID INDIA DZ DIG E443-LF-T-PC on CyberFace to Carrot Bay Intelligence from Moscow from Down Earth Motion Leaflet CFC Y79IIO - It got to Q1 to Q4 @ 200 Trillion $ (USD.SQ>NX.5000) T1000 $ UY KV-(5554300900W).

Peta O GP WAP Active Board Question was the success of confederacy. It got history recorded at 00:59 AM , 8 FEB 2021

Now a Constitutional MOC Move Challenged the PMO and President In India. I see that as Imperial B&W , an Introspective Block drew the square on CBI 55-H Mission. Files floated in Inbox from intenet.34worldwide@gmail.com . That was getting a C-Delta Infrared 4.00 CEO CFO Party Graph from Auckland 7 & Switzerland #E 3 GPU DOc X.006 For its First Mid Night Insertion at the Radio Factory for the entire range OP Cover on Economy. A 300 tier System Decorated the Constitution DQ Section IX and Sworn to POR Population -World Bank Digital CIP NETWORK --BI Task aimed to Cross 30 Trillion SEO Y670 @ 66.00 Ghzx From CHIP OU 8752407-NSDL Top Float-Radium DESK that could SAP CEO CFO CCFIO to Admin the ERT 5400 Billion USD (ETUOP.90) .

Today this is not my volley court vision for the world...you know it is the Pseudo Bond Partition...But this is our wall. I close saying it on my Hip Hop Station -Poland Gave XI KV a Clif Staff Merit -It was a IPS, IAS FederoX my name read on Facebook as KV Singh- The Entry was to Crew a Scientist Reader in Bot CPU SW 530 - H-W Rate of Bullion TOP LINE - It would alter Industry , labour and Common Man - Now you go and scoop a Number Chain.

CHAPTER FIVE

Angel To America

I decided the USA HY 5 for my UNFOLD ...it was New York , Street 5E to Washington DC. A light pipe spread over 100 Million Wire Solutions. RD 5.0 , JH 6.9 and WQ 3.7 were Non-Traded Sections K Dot Space Printing Ports, they fired the 400 Trillion EURO/AUD - POUND STERLING -00200060043000 on PNB Blue One from DB Google.GDS.XZA7Q by a Bolivian Court FCD 430-P to TAX Ensemble RIST Cash of YG 5000 B Yen - LP FD FEDERAL Vault was due for my spending occupation of a 300 Billion USD //INR-T = 500.9000 Crores In Citibank Inc , URTEFZX Search Park XE5500-9917 - My Name on Card -Karanvir Singh.

Wood we sat on ...we forgot CIA would flood latest bought encryption NATO DATA from its UN EDW was a Oblivion Discussion. It took her 300 Seconds. I stroked the Table and walk loaf in 30 Seconds. Fisher was Moved.

From my earth station where I frequently used my two-wheeler it nearly took me the LAME 5 Perfection to loop by March 2021- Arc Construction Knocked out Assets. It would be a 500 Trillion $ FGHT Estimation Post FJS 3000 on Global TECH COMPOST YE4300K -O090R.

Reclusive to temperature I found no normal ways to subside and dub my travels during in the period when I could not see the Treble working on the order. There a protocol XCF Denial On President was accumulated in Tendency to punish and vignette the cross-section. I am trooper , a boolean, a batch from 1987-89. My felicitation brought along a crop of disguised proponents who couldn't win the moment as it was happening. There was a wait for a call.

10 February, 2021| 21:05 PM

Library side was half negative and half promising to acquire many more positive results from the tests. The benchmark of medicine was getting pulled from eternal elevation to a sacred effect from it by side. When I took the jolt of getting dis-heartened it was heat and desert and a whole lot of pragmatic functions I could not just relate to but my mind fell asleep on the aircraft.

I wanted it immediately , I wanted a number on file to be retested and sent back from secretariat. That was a day on stroll. Choked I felt , resumed work and incapsulated internal security.

The check on Police was beneficial for the strong presence of calling it duty men and the servers of feasible protection to me.

I clocked many of the transitive cycles, held transition as subliminal and quoted the last testament that I discovered during my one recyclable visit to Colaba in South Bombay. It was a grasp checking out foreign visitors on holiday and label the strong form association with there immaculate culture to understand mine.

My compatibilty to compare the strongest face on earth ever to have been was my own plethora. Not Ego, But Ego Substantiated. A self wandering, Job... and a Love affair sold to barricades , trumpets,abuse and incitement for an unexcited young tablue.

BlueFedFin Ixc started me in 2013-14 ...it was red line , talk time , yellow telco, mint on demand and tress-passers not aloud.

I can label these adjectives and quantify the million tags that go reserved to occupy the world. With that density I could not move a single unit of expression not setting the lost list of transaction made while on a salaried position. The Bentley Dream....The Drive to Bombay and the exographic zone that I was able to demonstrate in the Public at Cafes , Walks and Joints could only be memorized if I say I did live the rouge and the foggy retreat to win over our Kingdom.

I stepped out once again and told party on a secured occasion that I m trying another changer. Game Changer, Goal Changer, Fate Changer and Fault Changer...Oh That was slow to solid scrum. Finally I came to Punjab in Mid-June volunteering the Light Lift from Airport and started hushing towards depression and unawarded brents from a side line of intricate wall the people around me had made. Depression was a new hope, It was happiness in a small cup , a single jar, cookies and sewed bitterness.

Kapple Kappe SXCi came to foray in 2015-16 , but I had to find the roots from my awakening in the limecast. Not for most of the challenge I could pen it. But I made it the digital way. Our first Section was written and I also occupied a political persona to identify myself a the legal developer of the legislation targeted at Business, Industry and Auto Crafting out of Plum Invention and Innovation. Excellence could it have been if the proposal was layered in the secret envelope to dance on the defence . It became a full-fledged networked hybrid security type market exchange that went functional in the coming years.

Exemption of interest in the present market scenario and

unintended pitch to strongly conclude a fresh era from a new age was to melt down rules from parity to check fresh ideas of how my companies were going to be classified.

Ixc was chosen for BlueFedFin as Internet Experience Company, SXCi for Kapple Kape as Secure Exchange Company Intelligence.

Then came iVDX and IPXi and XCi ....

The wonder came alive on the web , the default rate followed by Transmission was the biggest achievement on Planet. For myself and those who were in the elevator onto the confederation newly found adventure could not be resolved in the simplest term saying Thank You. The lord's will it came at a price not calculated but risked in awareness and dumped into unexpected price target to call them Liquefied Unadulterated Economic Supplies ... It was money ...but what kind of money ...a digital vault...a an AI GOLD RUSH ...and a High Priority Protocol to Fix and Dress Poverty.

Yes I took poverty to myself as subject and species for reclamation , drama and trauma. Touring the sub-divisons of those affected by the un-enterprising role of whoever into transacting at par with common man. I graduated from the concept to accord the rest of the sorority and felt it FED in my Files ...The Central Banks I could furnish... the Reserves of Prices and Bonds and Trades and what not in the Market.

A universe secured to transcend to a horizon of what could be the largest bubble in the so called increment. Oh I saw it says it went down and it went up. I Saw infinti , song unsung, a clap performed and a dream unbeaten.

Yes there were the bird heavens ...the bullet proof mechanical gates ...the escalade that I said is mine , the infringement that I conquered and the loss that I resolved.

My identity was a man in bread and slices... I showed what was inside the Golden Gates and what was in there in that Dolphin Channel that swam in the Blue Green Waters , hazzy, drowsy and goofy.

I herald the music lovers the makers of hip hop, rock and electronic...the mention that I first accounted a Diploma In Audio Engineering and then revamped the lateral studies was just not by chance. I can fix a calculator, belong to a PC, Draw a Workstation, Configure a Server , Paint a Sheet , Bend a Typhoon ...Like it was in the Sun Closet while I first shook that habit and blew away my masters advice. He said in a happy tone , I wont return but I will frontline your command as the holiest of holy. It was one promise I stole and cheered up on days I went and sat in the Hotel Lobbies...obscured the abstract of genuine revolt and KREEP (A Multi Faceted Blue Hybrid Currency Pole) was invented in year 2018.

KREEP- Works semi-numetic values and transitions from secure and safe money vaults that flow on the workspace and is a channel driven swift encrypted cloud allocation liquidity permanently placed in the AI and CODE Class called KRTPxCI 12000 and can have a Satellite Link, an Air Show and a Drive on Mobile , Notebook and can SCAN an IP of Variable Strength without Causing interruptions and hacks on anyone.

To go into further details I sorted what would be the Transaction Module , our innovation was as -

EPFXAr- 10.9987 (At Par)

Below Average Product Leaf- 6000

F-IP - @ ee.ii.pp.ll.ds.cloud.nucleus256/2802

G-Rate- 1.0006657 at a 900 % Mid Scale Output Docked to True Blue as Registered Component in the World.

H-UDSC-K - Was compared to IFSC standard at 100 Bullet

Points and 400% of the ATM Cross-Section Server amount was a Packet of 300 Million Mega Bounds for around 4000 Trillion in KREEP.

I-Ledger Maker IPMNYTx 9.0- Deployed the basic co-ordinates at a 360 degree value to cover choice load once I use the KREEP to Buy an ITEM.

J-Service-Blue COMyX - Served to Client Association and Customer Channel Proposed to Take over KREEP to WorldWide Audience in Mid of 2021 or at Least by JULY 9. Bedrock of surprise, bulletin watch on the drinks club...a few naughty balls...a bare stand at public again and those who were begging. I chose the smallest bit , the highest price and Pride to not only say I can do it alone and they were immensely supportive. I can't say that to Kearf Xeary's excellence maintained as Bot-Robo Controller Incharge of an email id on Google , but that was intrinsic out of the many benefits of the world of Radiation.

CHAPTER SIX

When Destiny Awaits

My NATO release of the edition was apprehensive and short. I could only say to the website to comply to my main motive. Be Secret and be Severe to Defaulters. I laid that justice in snowboarding from Shimla back to Punjab to Mumbai on several occasions and through my early years.

Where could India go from here, Not just mind to my own birthplace but if that someday sounds stupid will fault my generation and the enemy I saw . I am a cripple , too stupid not to say wise. I doesnt harm us in no way. Empathy, Sympathy and Agony are Child Roots of acquired harmony from nature. There the enemy id GOD. There the pulse to save I also GOD. I am that which never turns fade on phone and features.

SO here a future resounded victory bells and I stayed on the roof to present my endorsement to flex the world ..this entire planet was devised on my attribution and I looked once again to those green solid arms that I thought must be phantom and glory. Oh they were, naive be those who still couldn't hear or see it. Yell...Yell and that Fell.

CHAPTER SEVEN

Electrons on INSIPIAN 247

Wild as Lion, Our Alpha was 3000K , I was charging Space Discovery to get closer to my anxiety and curiosity ...It was who imagined it and who created it. My factorization from an IaaS and IPaaS aspiration with iOS and then to use NUcLEON OS a Graphic ON Index Changer Crawled me using a web space to create the Project called INSIPIAN 247 . That needed a Space Director , myself as CEOXCO Space and Solarizer . I counted till 99 assumed the responsibility to fix that junction , It was at my home base and then at Amritsar with the prayers. Combat design was fired and shot at sky ..Normalized the payload ...image from satellite got me thinking strong and bold .
Concave and Convex an eye line saw that. Narrow Engagement with a Senior Pilot, where is that house ?
I'm an internet buff. I am unable to change my habits...So where is the Cloud?
While inside the man -brain there were 10 Possible Used Transactions, I thought about the Trillions. In memory,blue and intelligent emissions. Transmitting A Signal A Light. That was electron bias. The foremost Theory in HBC. Human Body Communication.

Well noted by my campaign notes ...I had got worried about this miracle.

Graduate Hunting was basically trying to pull the PHd and then acquire new skills.I never felt so overwhelming To stop the non sense I had to supply support to the Dublin Farms. AI was cutting through since a 1000 Years. I was talking to INDIA. When you fetch a 1vR? Like! Quantum Science today relies heavily on moving particle theory.That must have been a secure bit cure. Hello Dr.KV, My Bit Coin. I got to pronounce my name as Karanvir Singh. HEDGE FUNDS OF 520 Billion £, Test Site Germany. Now when the pool goes as if empty incarnation brings world wide resources to match...why is everybody not reclusive? In an opinionated world every President must think Vibe and Channel. The secret laid before secret. It's an untwisted story. Tell me at .. 100.98.76.54 my IP Ha Ha... "Dr , KV Singh. The morning they charge that name is they go miracle."

My template CPU 2 CPU is now a mix of RAM Super Wire and a 100 Trillion Language Processing CHIPs on Hire. We sound a bit late but hey that's a habit...it's X Habitat...it Leonine.. Why would I back down from the hexa community laws. I will win the end and surprise the Fair n Fate Medicine. The tropical of hash tag mechanism in my book The Last Light of God was a pretty close call on believing God the one real entity of superposition in the tangent remarks of entire mankind and species. I had an order signed by self to percolate from the funnel the granules of free thought and free medicine.

Why else is the world a Ying Yang? Why is the world then dying...it's a high Contextual Point to roll out human misery n compare it to a malfunctioning Company...you got bad employees , bad working resources and possibly a bad working Bank.

How should I have taken the oath is two parts of a paradox yet to be featured on the best-selling magazines and known hot selling New Media.

I mean HBC, Human Body Communication was there in theory. Way to go...but here I relate to it...

Blue Light coming in the near field...what is it??

Miracle!!!

Have I now found the feeling from my adorable sanctity...

I keep a spouse, a kid and a meal.

I m just the Single Phantom ... Surprise...at the door!

InSipiaN you are creating an atmosphere not existing before. I thought cosmic invasion is still a proof of advertising. I m advertising.

I buying a solid state disk and a SATA Drive to rewrite history...I will only include the 1 Bit Intelligence and the 24 Mega Byte if knowledge was the heroic in the entire history of the homi sapiens.

Homo Sapiens , 128 Bit SSL. Ha Ha!!!

InSipiaN 247 drops a message to the International Space Station... Dr. KV onboard...I was still laughing...where is the space suite...is there laughing gas on it...

I m sure the biggest industry profiles are just the same as the Polynomial answer to the square root of 20 and 2000..

Binary 2 is 2020 ...is that the Covid 19 Presence. No the human null n void theory.

Any Accessible acceptance is normally ruled out...we are insufficient now.

We could create the island of hope...we could start the war before it's too late.

Cosmos is weeping so silently that it would raise our dead from fumes and bones...a light of God to hold the truth upright and not let anyone crucify our mercy.

CHAPTER EIGHT

Secret To Surprise

Every time the HBC (Human Body Communication) idea came to my mind I was expecting a video recording for it. Or a secret Would remain a secret.

There are many cubes many IC-e Cubes.

Every thing connected to everyone. My attempt to classify the hottest discovery ever on earth.

"When the rain turned green I realized it was a rough patch between me and the code I was looking for. It really Requires a multi fold imagination to capture the holistic idea of truth and the penetrating depth of Truth."

Why I realized a gross command exists is because I don't hang out with a bunch of morons.

Welcome Back!

I doubt if there is a solo particle that is responsible for the creation of the Universe. But one such particle is the deaf Impact of unnatural Acquisition man has grown up with.

It's called nonsense. Non sense is identified as two yellow and one brown mental codes. People who do it cannot be encrypted for the secret recipe denies the publication of a behaviour that aggressive. I am charging my phone. Do you realize how much ink that is...??? Well while you find the answer to this dialogue I have a few preferred connotations on the ministry of non sense. Some people go fry their brains in the heat....song-like ....bird-lake...Some fetish around lakes and beaches and like ignorance and indeed are rich with that phenomenon.,that phenomenon....that One....ha Ha...You shipped the code to me. I was meeting a new oracle star ... when that happens I will come sit by your side and touch all love inside your craftiness.

Well done Colonel!! Oh Kernel Missing FRIX!!

Who?

FRIX!!

Let me take you on a flight with me...the international outcry made me a war hero...how ? You gotta realize it...I still remember making the Team reach a higher Computing Providence than earlier. This was Cloud Blue Live. It was discovered in a days time...then made to work with anticipation and it acquired the pensive nature of an electronic ion in the Virtual Space. CBL 5000 ,CBL 1000 ...they all applied to mathematically assigned Virtues and did fail n succeed. The failure was a nap ...and the success was the wakefulness of the intended internet results from the Meta Force behind CBL which gave us EncRypto 1.1.1313.

I would not forget coming to office before time and leaving at late hours putting all the trust in the Cloud and making ends with a meteorite jam in my cell phone.

Greatly every lesson was told as if the teacher was angry at surprise...full of genius...Frix Text was a solo invention like the many others...there was some resemblance between my natural instinct as Frix made to Stage 1 of the experiment.

I note this down on a stone face scarlet clown ...we are really great people ..the humanity is outlandish. Its so cruel when a bebo-boy says he's got nothing from the shower.

It was 9 PM Friday , I was searching for a few text messages and I couldn't match a flight to support the argument. There it fell under the tree support and I recognized a fair amount of hard work put in all through a decade of astute deliverance and a hopefull fry match to a lovely verdict.

God heard what I said...God ?? Oh Yes its a system that resembles high tides. A cyclone a tsunami!! But within the computing world I gave a grim chance to inner beauty, grabbed the tree and viola what a feat of magical spells.

Who would say a light bean would emerge from the memory to directly speak to my wireless antenna. I am happy for all reasons. I am always happy for no reasons.

The quantum push came from the presentations I drew on my Helium 12...Its a series of Paper Blue Isx. A digital intervention company I imagined in the grass. The Yellow Grass!!

Why would it take 30 Million Cognitive function and 1000 Billion Neurons involved in making the transition from signal to signal.

I am marketing two possible side products...one is Robots and the other is ofcourse Humans. Human for Human and A Robot for Human. This may get translated. The Robot would finish the work from Atom to Atom and the Human would be over joyed by Yoga!! What a surprise my robot taught me two principles ...one; never be ignorant and two ; be cautious with knowledge.

These are not the world commands but rather simple astonishing questions. Why are we still a poor state when it comes to economics? I consider the poverty of Robot. He hasn't been given the best circuit that he chose. Rather the human choice is an ethereal axiomatic presence on earth.

As humans the secret to surprise came from early creation myths...who would tell them who brought them here and gave them money to run the world.I am sitting on CBDC and Crypto...

The Hash Tag that came supposedly was just a number...a number 442. Who would gamble a card on it...may be the credit card company I work with will assume the money is there and then I don't pay my dues. But hey I am not asking to be defaulters but responsible mates.

Is that we look beyond courage? Or do we look at mass carnage as the most beautiful thing alive. We gotta separate ourselves from money and brim up talent, hard work and artistry.

An Artisan once paired the grip of his shoes and said which one is harder...answer? The one touched is harder.

Now I have two small blue-tooth device and hard part I don't know which one pairs on what code. When I see the light beam transmission and see that blue light I don't understand whats going one. Ha ha...my hind brains knows and I am not talking to him.

That should not get worse that which is protected by God.

Here a tip; when you charge your ear buds pay attention ...its using your electricity.

CHAPTER NINE

White Matter & Blue Matter

"Human consciousness is at the behest of artificial knowledge a man attains during his lifetime. What he get as nutrition is what he work to will. 21st Century is ruled by AI and other supernatural discoveries. I am not mocking it you see. Don't laugh untill the mansion clears the joke. The woody goodness of mankind has been stolen into the computers. The mainframes are my first love. The Software , the white matter ,is the steak invention of human entropy. I would further suggest that we cant argue to the POS that delivers your Ledger. The banking industry has witnessed a global conundrum of ethos. I like the cultured world and on my side I have very few targeted humans who understand the probability of a round earth. Lets go around it. Lets absorb the sun and what are we left with? The ionic matter the white shades turning orange and red and then the blue matter......
I saw a dream that day...the richest man in the world and then the other day the wisest among men.

By the side of women an encrypted cos-sine combination does work.

I am a dreamer no cause dreamer but a real amphitheatre of the globe. The other day I discussed a bunch of apples with my team ...they said its okay but how would you eat the last one..I said I am not hungry. The team met the coincidence within the paradox and I ate the apple. Are there Apple Pie Charts??

So Victory here!!

The blue matter is interesting in many ways and many folds...its reaches the pleasure senses and appeals to the mind and the mind within the mind. So jealous of your cards!!

Lets talk about the geometrical shapes...hey its there in the moment of inertia. External consciousness is great awareness and I cant live without it. Do you consider only torque...its called spinning the wheels and making a concord rush out into blue sky.....white clouds.

Where there is necessity there is a need to adopt new ways...to function on axis I believe we have one God and one human life.God doesn't calculate the perpendicular distance...he's there at the starting line and there at the finishing end of the miracles He Knows.This is kind of motion and the light splits in few micro seconds.

Matter does matter in the matter of mindful exoneration and outcast suspension. The ether is free and White & Blue are always there in the dream."

CHAPTER TEN

Cognitive Receptors

All components of all kinds of forces bow down before us..and when is see an axis getting blue its makes me a thunderbolt in the eyes of the rest of mankind.
Why is the cross product zero??
We don't realize in our daily routines ..how much we spend on buoyancy for equal resources. Equality is the edge of cognition.. it should be mandatory to revise an old syllabus and jump into the New Age.Would you invite Archimedes? Oh Yes!!
FRIX likes him....he saved him from drowning.
Now here and there we all venture out with ease of doing business as smart as the web and there we see our principle states of mind acting on a trillion receptors inside the brain.The shop open at 9 and shuts down at 9. Consider the figure getting bigger and fluid...how do they act on liquidity when the equity falls below the targets. We over use...we use & throw and we measure the vessel as empty. Someone gotta fill it to the top.
Substituting the boundaries of human endeavors by a mean value of the polyatomic molecules is therefor arranged in the fashion that secretly leaks the repulsive force. Nuclear forces acting inside the mind ...its not so jumbled...each one of us is a bundled pair of electrons...then nucleons..the

rabbit hole is deeper than anyones imagination. The crux of atom is God himself at the beginning and at the end of creation.

Do you believe in an ionic bond??

Ha ha..

- A cohesive force ...an adhesive force!! Where do they all go for shower? Hah!! The news makers of the world are at equilibrium.An equilateral suspense..but I am on the safe side of it...To all my teachers I owe my surface tension, my own enigma...my very nature to produce and protect the carnival.
- Its a festival of over joy and ultimate peace of mind...this peace of paper is sold on basis. The Basis of your knowledge is this one paper greatly depressed and ambient. The score of words and my total points are both not Zero (0).

"This translates parallel to itself. I am yearning to see God in Cognition. My receptor says 001010F 0101F!!"

My internal forces are no more conservative.

Are you listening to the Radio??

CHAPTER ELEVEN

The Aura Of Work

After a decade long overhaul and a steady halt of 7 years I realized somewhere this new invention would be parked in the best of the worlds dilemma. It takes huge for a HBC worker and I cant forget to mention my own complicated inertia.

We all ground ourselves and pitch dark entry in the realm of digital cosmos...we are initially at the centre of the universe and there the stars arise within the dream of the piper..

The centre of mass is your diluted peg of tropical summer boots and you do like to split the time by nano seconds.The working habit around HBC and other root of internet fundamental potential is greatly bright shining atmosphere.

1. There is the redshift....and the doppler and the acoustic chamber is laden with queries and multi million dollars of capacitance and liquid show buzz. How would you park your car here?

2. If we stay in the same position we would regret not knowing such a phenomenon. Not knowing how gazing at the sun made the mind a solar active computer and a half degree epitome of the most wonderful thing ever on earth.

The contact angles and the tangent planes are inevitable evidence of the invention.

<u>Do want to see a polar bear?</u>

No not in the Arctic...here right on your shoulder.

While a lot of aspects of how the discovery unleashed itself is what I assume to be my culmination of the thesis.

Here we equally pledge and devote our time to what we study, apprehend and conceive in the mind.

A little convenience is the media especially radio companies getting wild in the socket.

<u>Less liquid...less Fragile...A Bottle of Wine!!</u>

CHAPTER TWELVE

Western Miles & Games

I remember I got interested in the American media and the American Politics towards the end of 2007...I was not aware of the offices but did know how they choose a President.

I re looked at my plans and once introduced myself as the icon of unity...that was boasting meant to proceed to the gates.

AN exuberant thing in life has been my melody to sing in the dark days but yeah it takes a rap to snap the hip hop.This was a usual tier and I acclaimed most of the fame through the window called internet radio.

- Now where do I belong ? To history a mark of advice ...what I said is regal and royal...it has to be felt in the presence of articulation...deep mathematical knowledge and greater scientific agility.
- Tranquility is divine and the divine is a sea-scape made to know God...A life full of prose and wine is equally everyone's share.

- The mild tribulations in the house of sacred knowledge is an outdated practice and I believe there is broad range of spectrum that can guide us to follow the ultimate dream. The One World Order- Or a one united world.

On the front of a war if I send two hundred soldiers to combat I gotta give them fuel and plug.
What a melancholy? The devices today are more than your imagination ...yet we cant disfigure our proportion of truth in our minds and in our hearts. Our hearts shall thus now the evident future and repair the past and slide to the jumper setting and crib only if required.

The miracle does work and it fades at times but its the inner curiosity that leads to light and freedom.
The significant part of the world is development and I see that as a code breaker. Money is unlimited.
The precise moment to reach forward to profits must be an ethical record.

The cost of future is always Zero ...something everyone can afford.

The later is realized as the ultimate ground reality the Blue Miracle is there to stand by and eat the repository function.
No matter if this time the Apple falls on the side of inventory.
SO lets come forward and recognize technology as the leader of the crimson world. A world for all and a world for everything and for everyone. This is one message which would recall in our minds about how and why a man discovered Enigma and shook the world. Its Encryption...Its call the Advent of the NEW AGE A Golden

AGE!!

Epilogue

Whatever one does in life is sufficientyly the truth of his being.Man is an inerted and inverted candidate and a psychopath. I believe one day when robot take over our work they will choose the toughest passwords. Then it might be true that God exists as One. That day would be Encrypted in a Psygram!

Thank You !

About The Author

"As long you stay in the Entrepreneurial Domain You are the Main Actor and the main Subsidy of the Business Undertakings. This time I have a magical wand and I am interested in blowing away phantom and force to the industry & the ministry.

Anti-phishing Laws and the truth behind the ceremonial walls. Better value supply and the Side Chain Method of Developing Scientific business ideas and calculating upon Integrity and Technological advancement vis a vis the New World Order.

I was born in Amritsar and I am 33 Years Old and this happens to be my turning instance of the moment to surprise everyone with an Institution Par Excellence.

As long you stay in the Entrepreneurial Domain You are the Main Actor and the main Subsidy of the Business Undertakings. This time I have a magical wand and I am interested in blowing away phantom and force to the industry & the ministry.

Anti-phishing Laws and the truth behind the ceremonial walls. Better value supply and the Side Chain Method of Developing Scientific business ideas and calculating upon Integrity and Technological advancement in the New World.

I am 33 Years Old and this happens to be my turning instance of The moment to surprise everyone with an Institution Par Excellence."

Applause

Carrot InteLLIO - ***** Encryption is a Blockbuster!
Paper Blue -***** I900 Global Blue Bestseller!
KapeSine -***** INQ 6000 Bestseller- Encryption Steals The Show!
All Rights Reserved.